The Underwritten Plain

Also by Tim Metcalf and published by Ginninderra Press

Corvus

Cut to the Word

Into the No Zone (Highly Commended,
2004 ACT Publishing Awards)

*Verbal Medicine: 21 Contemporary Clinician Poets
of Australia and New Zealand* (Winner, Poetry,
2007 ACT Writing & Publishing Awards)

The Solution To Us (Shortlisted, Poetry,
2009 ACT Publishing Awards)

The Effective Butterfly

Red Song of the Red Earth (Pocket Poets)

Tim Metcalf

The Underwritten Plain

The Underwritten Plain
ISBN 978 1 76041 577 8
Copyright © Tim Metcalf 2018
Cover photograph: Tim Metcalf

First published 2018 by
Ginninderra Press
PO Box 3461 Port Adelaide 5015 Australia
www.ginninderrapress.com.au

Contents

To the reader	9
I	11
II	25
III	43
IV	57

'How many do we know of who have fled from the sweetness of a calm life at home among people they knew in order to undergo the horrors of uninhabitable deserts, throwing themselves into conditions abject, vile and despised by the world, delighting in them and going so far as to prefer them!'

Michel de Montaigne (1533–1592)
Essays 1:14

To the reader

This poem is set at the Albala-Karoo bore, which today is nothing more than a hole cut in the Nullarbor plain. One rusted strand of wire hopefully suffices to warn the passer-by. Nearby are some abandoned yards, an old highways department water tank, and a headstone for one Herman Johnson. In 1992, an optical fibre cable was laid alongside. No one has stayed here for a long time, and visitors are few.

The site is in South Australia, about 60 kilometres east-north-east of Eucla, along the old highway surveyed in the late 1800s by Ernest Giles and others. The limestone plain, known as karst from the type site in Slovenia, is undercut with a largely unmapped cave system. The Aboriginal people believed that the great creation snake they called Wonambi moved through the desert using these conduits. The cool air blast from these caves and natural vents in the plain on the hottest of days was Wonambi's breath. The nearby Koonalda cave contains some intriguing diagrams dated at 22,000 years.

I have used the tribal names published in the local histories, but no one, I think, really knows what the first people called themselves. I have tried to imagine what the people might have said and thought, drawing upon my visits to the place, my own contact with Aboriginal people around Australia, and the early 20th century anthropological notes we are fortunate to have from the Ooldea area, especially the writings of Daisy Bates and the masterwork by R.M. and C.H. Berndt, *The Speaking Land*.

Here at the southern limit of the Nullarbor, Australia ends

in sudden cliffs that plummet a hundred metres or more to form the clean curve of the Great Australian Bight. The poem begins imagining the first person to ever see this abrupt and spectacular end to the vast stone slab that is our continent.

Tim Metcalf

I

Mirning know the stories, Mirning speak the dreaming.
Wongai tell their stories the right way.

But hey what's this? We need a story here!
Kangaroo's journey finished here!

Wombat was turned back here!
Dingo could not run around this place!

Like ants at the waterhole's edge, we cannot see across.
It smells of salt and the sound of thunder does not end.

Wonambi lives down those holes.
Have Mirning found his secret home?

Mirning will find the names for this place.
Mirning will find the way to the water.

At Koonalda our fathers went down.
Into the earth, they went down to meet the snake.

Moon man did not follow them to light their way.
In the snake's breath, the torch burnt down too fast.

They left some signs, but not their meaning.
They sprayed some ochre, but could not see their hands.

They said they did not meet Wonambi.
They said they felt its chill breath closer.

They left us after that, to follow Emu's track.
My father's father left with them, to find the right story.

I tell the stories they left with us.
I cannot tell those they took away.

Wonambi showed the water where to flow.
Our elders followed on their journey.

Here it tunnelled underground,
swallowing Mirning, swallowing stories.

Our wise men given stories in return –
we must protect them.

Our women given children in return –
we must protect them.

Black hole, white ochre.
Here we sit and sing.

And when the song falls away
we breathe in, and start again.

Does Wonambi visit all the places, or
is there a baby giant snake for every hole?

Is this one its home,
that big creation snake that made the land?

So many questions, my father laughs.
'I will speak the name. Then you speak it.'

All snakes are water, they slip
over the land, and inside it.

Wherever they are flowing to
they make the same sound.

Their children can kill dingoes
with a baby bite.

At Koomooloobooka my father spoke all the names.
I was too young to be given the secret ones.

Every hole Wonambi made has its place name.
The cold breath tells you where this giant is!

My names for where the country falls away
are 'white lip of the stone ghost', and

'great waterhole of the dreaming beings
where they wash until they are as black as sky'.

I whispered these to my woman and she laughed.
Now she is asleep, and dreaming.

She is smiling! Lying down, on her side,
the new moon in her sleeping mouth.

In the flat land, a black hole.
Here strange stories come for me.

Willy-willies emerge to wander the world.
No one has been taken for a long time.

Burning stones fly from the sky.
Water pools, in the pits they make.

The moon is a bad man.
His bad medicine visits us at night.

But he is too old to chase young women.
He rears then eats his dingo pups.

Suddenly the snake's head fills the hole!
A child taken will later be regurgitated.

The ones who are lost are returned to us,
through the blood-fringed passage of woman.

I wonder, did Wonambi take my father?
Was it the snake that swallowed his stories?

It threw his white bones back up.
Strewed them around its hole.

Bats are the blowing ashes
of the words he left us.

When the snake's tail flicks
I jump out of the way!

It flicks and vanishes up
into that big hole in the stars.

Father said the snake must eat.
It is why the dingoes howl at dawn.

He did not return from his journey.
He stayed in the sky with sun woman.

I ask him should I feed the snake?
With a corpse, with that Wongai who fought us.

Will he be good for Wonambi's guts?.
Must that snake's food be alive?

Father you left with that story.
What names should I pronounce outside your cave?

Father, return to me in dream.
Tell me what to do?

The white man has cut a new hole.
'That's my bore.'

Wonambi can be felt and heard.
Wonambi must be fed.

The initiate boys must bleed
at the stone lip white with ochre.

They must not cry out
when we lower them head-first and laugh.

They must not cry out
when we cut them and say nothing.

Silence! Respect for the ancestors!
Silence! Wonambi will swallow you whole!

My arm is fractured from the fight.
We fought about the bore hole's story.

That Wongai said it's not the living burrow
but the throat hole of the snake turned stone.

But he is from a distant country.
He does not know our stories of the bore.

This place is called Albala-Karoo.
My father told the stories of this place.

I am guarding those stories.
I would not give that Wongai any stories.

He cannot take them from me.
'Get your own! We'll push you down that throat!'

The white man says he crossed the water.
He says he saw no snakes in it.

But whose breath do we shiver in
at his bore hole's margin?

I fear I will be leaping
into the snake's open mouth.

If I jump in. White man gave me drink
he says to make my courage grow.

At Koomooloobooka will I re-emerge
to laugh together with my anxious people?

The white man is laughing like a crow.
'Find someone else to go!'

II

Tietkin stayed on. I brewed fine tea.
He smoked, I carved '1890'.

The bore was drilled. At the fire
I won at cards: three rolls of wire.

Tops for fencing, and my third roll!
He didn't like my highway toll!

Two mates with him won him over.
'Where's the fun in staying sober?'

But I never got to know 'em –
they've departed from my poem.

There's only me for fifty miles
camped on the track of Ernest Giles.

Let's make a note here, right away.
I'm not the poet of the day.

I'm just a poet of the plain.
To lit'rature my work's no gain

and out here I can plainly see
my audience comprises me.

One couplet short of a sonnet?
Let's not extemporise upon it.

If in error I steal a rhyme
well honestly I thought it mine.

My name will never grace a shelf
so I can write to please myself.

'Herman Johnson, Now You're Gone Son'
I'd have engraved upon his grave.

I will think up witticisms
as I eat the sheep brought with him

night after night, day after day
(he left last year, he couldn't stay).

I laugh with Herman, as if I'm crazed,
or overheated, in a haze

or too vague, like the horizon,
indefinite, in the great heat

like this meat with clouds of flies on
that I was keeping for next week.

First up, the fence. Know where I stand.
Clear to the sheep, clear to native man.

But if there's trouble from the tribes
in my trunk I have some bribes

for expenses, and violence
to defray. It's common sense.

It makes sense too to have some fun,
and even more to clean your gun.

I'll string it tight but not too tense.
I have to sleep behind this fence.

So like my verses not too strained,
the animal within unchained.

Introducing the right angle!
Introducing barbed wire tangle!

Scrape your knuckles on the limestone.
Burn your fingers on the grindstone.

My sheep companions bleat and cough
when drinking from the water trough –

the only way they know to thank
the white men for their water tank.

Now I've my tent, yards halfway made,
a track from Perth to Adelaide

I think I'll be a trading post –
cull money from the passing host!

Just as well I'm no top poet
'cos there's no one here to know it.

Though I can't write a proper poem
at least I've written something down

though there is almost nought to tell:
the farming life is going well.

My horse is hale, my sheep will sell
(although they scamp about pell-mell)

Perhaps I'll hang a mission bell.
Then this place would be pure hell!

Laugh, cry, now bravely write this down:
I miss Mathilda in her gown.

Out here to meet myself at last.
Myself, away from all my past.

Yet my head swarms with old stories.
Foolish ones. No wars, no glories.

Is it madness to name each tree
after people dear to me?

My friends who yearned to roam so free?
My friends who helped me cross the sea.

I ran away from wedding cake.
I fled for sweet Mathilda's sake.

No one will ever find me here.
I can relax. Dismiss my fear.

Great Prince of all that I survey!
If I upend my throne of hay

and climb up onto the new roof
then I'm the King, and stand aloof

from this plain, the Nullarbor
and our saviour Tietkin's bore.

From camel trains (and soon the rails!)
or from the ocean's passing sails

the lease belongs to none but me
as any traveller can see.

And far from priests, all that's phoney,
the blacks maintain their ceremony.

The dingoes think they are rehearsing
the Wongai songman's song of cursing

that falls down and away like life
from the lamb, after the knife.

At first I had old Europe's habits.
I didn't understand the rabbits

and sheep and cows and all the rest
could overgraze. The farm's a mess.

The crows are waiting on the plain.
The eagles treat me with disdain.

I am the king of all this land.
My dominion. My scarred hand.

The blacks spread white ochre, the bore
is iced like a cake, and what's more

it's like marriage, best forgotten,
a black hole without a bottom!

Nearby a struggling stand of trees
like headdresses shaking leaves

looks like spirits caught in flight
from our dawning nation's light.

With the relentless wind they try
to flee the ground, uproot and fly

to where? The new world's so unkind.
I'm happy to be left behind.

Some nights I clutch my Bible tight,
imagining it combats fright.

The book I fled here to avoid!
Sometimes I'm scared, a little boy!

I fear knocking, sudden, violent –
but if it's blacks, they'll be silent.

They fear a snake in the bore.
I fear their spears at my door.

And I dread them when they're angry,
and, from what they say, when hungry.

All of which is foolish and blind:
A wise man fears his own kind.

The bore seems a lightning maker.
Lightning leaves us smoking craters.

There is nowhere to run from here!
Was it too much sugar in my tea,

or some secret tribal factor –
fencing wire is an attractor –

but I dreamt, one electric night
a black Mathilda called, in fright.

Her children would have hid outside
until up close the dingoes cried.

So there were four inside my gate –
and as I dreamed we grew to eight!

First it was shy. Twice I was bitten.
Now I love my little kitten.

My heart's truly über-smitten,
and the lease is underwritten!

This native girl, she loves the cat,
so I've two friends, and fancy that!

The bore invites the kangaroos,
so I invite her group for food.

They feast all night, I go to sleep –
and never have to count my sheep!

And then one morning I woke up
and found I owned a dingo pup!

I talk with birds, like St Francis
but with snakes I take no chances.

Human beings I think worse snakes
than the black's Wonambi, who makes

them jittery. When we came through
with sheep that time, then the bore crew –

no surprise they met us with spears.
But they soon overcame their fears.

Next, camel breath, tetchy horse, sweat-
soaked saddle blankets. And remorse.

The iron horse will ride this plain,
and they'll have learnt to ride in vain.

'Ark ark' the ravens near and far
are curious but wary.

They know that sometime I will die,
and my gun's no longer scary.

I have made small report. This land
has drained my pen and stilled my hand.

It hasn't rained, and never yet
did it – 'twas only drops of sweat

that I felt falling from the brim
of my hat, flung now to the wind

across the plain, a scrap of bark.
I ride. The raven's crow 'ark ark'.

III

It's only yards and a bore, mate.
Albala-Karoo. What does that mean?

I dunno. Bloody hole in the bloody ground.
Why don't you ask your cousin?

Who's my cousin?
Fire up the digger, mate.

Mate, it's a heritage site.
Bullshit.

And obviously sacred.
Mate, look around. No one gives a shit.

Treat it with respect, mate.
Yeah yeah. OK.

Mate, I wouldn't walk backwards.
That's how kangaroo and emu survive out here, eh.

Sinkholes in the limestone. They puncture the plain.
You could drop out of sight forever;

scratch us your signature on the way down.
Like the ones up the track there, at Koonalda cave.

I reckon that was the giant wombat.
They say it was religion or art.

What difference would it make out here, mate?
They're called 'intentional finger flutings'.

Cognitive Archaeology. It's on the internet.
If you dig deep enough!

Yeah, the bore hole breathes,
same as the caves, mate.

It's the temperature gradient.
Cool, eh?

Love my traditional air conditioning?
Problem is, you have to stand just here.

So, in the mind of early man
it could have been down there –

a cold-blooded reptile –
the dreamtime snake Wonambi?

Plenty of caves to hide in.
Keeping his head down since Maralinga, mate.

I would face the morning too.
It was 46 here yesterday.

In Memory of Herman Johnson.
Died 10th of December 1899.

He can't have known too much, at first.
The sun would have taught him quickly.

Why face the sun when you're dead?
It's about hope. Looking forward.

Be hard without any eyes, mate.
They did it all over the world.

Lord of all this, eh? Alive and dead.
What difference would it make out here?

What kind of white man would stay here
long enough to die?

The barbed wire has torn his story to shreds.
What this nail held fast is lost.

Oh, spare us the poetry, mate, it's hot today.
How do you know he was a white man?

Was he some kind of spirit being
to the Mirning? Good, or bad?

Good. Otherwise he would not have survived here.
Mate, he didn't survive here.

(At night the dingoes recall
a disquieting sense of loss.)

The Highways Department's sunken tank
is hidden by those prickle bushes

and beneath the bushes ravens
peer through the rusting bars.

The light tries to penetrate an algal bloom,
green and yellow. Into focus, slowly

oozed a round shape, floating
just beneath the surface. A soft flowering.

Mate, I saw it then. A nose,
and receding into the stagnant depths

the dingo's head, its eyes
staring from a putrid soup.

This is truly a lonely grave.
four thin rails and a stone.

A bullet wound beneath the date.
Strewn about, beaten tins

spark plugs, strands of wire,
timber weathered beyond all use,

the rubbish of a century
that nothing has yet evolved to eat.

The neat rectangle of the plot
is heaped with stone chips,

worked fragments of cave flints.
Herman has a buried message, mate!

Know your old bottles, mate?
Neat circle, eh?

They don't look that old.
Better watch that antiques show.

Bloody TV will be an antique
before you get that cable laid.

Dickheads from the city. Bloody OH&S.
I'll sweat to death in this shit they make you wear.

Cable'll choke up the day they switch it on,
there's that much crap talked in the world.

Leave the broken glass alone.
I'll take you into Eucla for a beer.

Old Herman will be busy, now we have laid
our cable to rest beside him.

Fibre-optic cable, coast to coast!
'From the cable to the grave'…

'Ark ark' as the ravens say,
killer humour, mate.

Day and night, millions of words
will flow past his underground ear

Yeah yeah, what's the marker number, mate?
2.7.6. underground river of light.

Poor Herman! He will be tormented
by all the babble he came here to escape.

Herman and the natives alike
would have taken fright at our modern sky!

Planes on a schedule. Satellites like stars
set free, to wander silently

never burning bright and crashing to the ground.
(Except for Skylab, mate.)

City folk cannot know the ancient night,
yet hold on to their fear.

Of what? For the first people
day was the hot shadow of night

comfortable night, when the food was cooked!
When singing by the fire began!

He had to be running
from something, or someone.

No way would the money
make up for life out here.

Mate you've been out in the heat.
Like a nervous roo, jumping to conclusions.

How do you know who he was, or how lonely?
There was always people passing through.

Giles' survey, Tietkin's bores, Eyre's highway.
Rail soon after. Now the cable's global traffic.

At light-speed it will pass Herman's door.
No time to stop and say 'Hello'.

Lights on late in the far city office.
Time to run the final tests.

Meanwhile, my mind just runs on out here
all by itself.

It's like a big diesel
with an endless fuel supply.

It's funny how all this nothing gets you thinking.
It's full of surprises out here.

Load the empty drums.
Load up the trench digger.

Two hours to Eucla. In the beginning, God made beer.
And what about women, mate?

IV

Black hole,
inkwell.

I dip my finger
into ancient

memory
oldest mind

make a circle
in the sand.

Red grains
make way

for beginning
and end.

'The lid blown off'
I call the moon

bone white reminder
of our destination.

The pockmarked face of the land.
Red sand scouring limestone.

Stone shadow
of the night sky

the mirror-moon
has fallen from its frame.

Beware the black hole
with the white ochre rim.

White ochre lights
the bore's southern lip

like new moon
demarcating

the old black
absence,

like a spelunker's lamp
illuminating underground

a tremulous arc
of the cavern wall

where stories are secreted
from the surface heat.

Don't go there!
Furtive dingoes

patient ravens
circle the silent shaft

the disc excised
from level ground.

Here depthless metaphor
is set in stone.

An absorbing book:
one falls through the pages.

Death will come for you.
There's no call to jump.

Dark well,
gravitational lens

for examining in depth
my fear. My deepest origin.

For magnifying
my loneliness.

Pinned already
to be dragged

to be spiralling in
to be holding my breath

hoping I will be spat out
on this side of the world.

Black hole
in the land.

Black hole
in the sky.

The first
is air

the second
dust.

In my head, in my eyes –
twin black holes reflect, reflect

yet consciousness
somehow exists.

Black hole
direct channel

to the subterranean,
to the unknown.

Black pupils,
all of our eyes

line the path
for light

so it may enter
our inner sanctum

our secret cave,
our bony skull.

They diamond-drilled here
into the doubters

of gravity,
of life.

We lifted water
from the earth.

We built a great collider
to drink deep

of the bubbling
youthful universe.

It was bursting
with energy and questions.

My black hole
is imperfect

information
is emerging.

Bats flitter out
like useless facts.

Insects are walking
up and down the walls.

Birds nest on
undercut shelving.

My metaphor generator
has audible ball bearings.

Invisible blades
Insatiable turbine

Falling bodies
Spin the machine

If I jump
It will charge another story up

'how I fell forever
and then emerged

into perfect happiness'
would be good

But if believable
I would not be standing here.

The bone-breaking land
is founded on space.

Decayed roots create conduits
for scorpions and lizards

The plains rat burrows,
rabbits warren

wombats excavate,
white man's hydraulics

and water dissolves
the limestone into caves.

Wormholes riddle the universe.
On what do we stand?

A silica cable
traffics our lives

through an ancient
ocean bed

past sinkholes
vast caverns

past lonely graves
abandoned homes

white-browed babblers
perched on greying timber.

Kindly the world's blather
flicks through at light speed.

Fibre-optic cable
flickering conversations

under my feet
photos, documents.

Above my feet my mind
cannot free itself

from what it knows.
The first people departed.

The stars have been numbered.
My generator synchronised

to the grindstone, galactic
motion in perpetuity.

Black hole
mother

an obvious
association

I was born
my story was born

mother
everyone was born

you were too.
What a dangerous stunt!

It is right that young men
should bleed at the edge.

The people
and their stories

tumble in.
The initiate blood

sprinkling red
the white ochre

full moon, cold night
sweat on their bodies

black moon
at their feet

regurgitating
their tales.

Moon was a man
chasing women.

Women were stars
running away.

Sometimes they tripped
and fell to earth.

Loud noise
when they hit the ground!

Maybe they wormed their way
deep underground

leaving us a hole
to skirt.

Moon man's
shadow head

lopped from his body
at ground level.

From the right place
on the right night

we can watch him
ascend

separate at the bore hole
from his black trachea.

Sing him back to sleep!
To assuage his power!

That story snaked
its way across the desert

until it came to
the continental edge

where its tail disappeared
down one of many holes.

The stories followed it
and the elders died.

Women, bring forth again
those wailing men.

Men, return to us
when you've grabbed that tail.

Worldwide, people left the caves
a long time back.

We are still painting
our fear on the walls

of great galleries, ours
in blazing light

and from the greatest light
the galactic core's black hole

the masterful vortex
is still dragging us

helpless against the infinite
back to ourselves.

Nothing is pure white.
The ochre's crystalline impurities

the white woman's
inner thigh

all my teeth
tobacco stained.

Nothing is pure black:
brave light

daring the bore hole
abseils the shaft:

trouble for my enemies
hiding in the dark.

Eerie pink, pre-dawn.
A weird mist.

Dingo calls
slip through.

One day's walk
from the southern ocean.

The dew so heavy
it can be drunk from leaves.

Sipping light
with water:

two ways to refresh
your waking thirst.

from
The Oxford English Dictionary
Second Edition
Volume XVIII

Underwriter †3a 1639 Wotton in Reliq (1651) 458:

I have now no more to say,
but that while the foresaid report shall be false
The underwriter is Truly yours

Tim Metcalf

www.ingramcontent.com/pod-product-compliance
Lightning Source LLC
Chambersburg PA
CBHW062148100526
44589CB00014B/1741